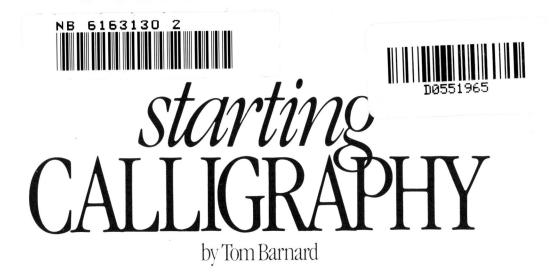

starting CALLIGRAPHY

by Tom Barnard

ISBN 1 871517 45 1

Osmiroid Creative Leisure Series

About the Author

Tom Barnard was born in London, where he trained as an art student and eventually entered the Royal College of Art. He studied calligraphy, book binding and allied crafts, and on obtaining his A.R.C.A. diploma taught in a number of art colleges in London and Kent.

A Fellow of the Society of Scribes and Illuminators, and Calligraphy and Handwriting Consultant to Osmiroid International, Tom has travelled over a million miles giving demonstrations of Calligraphy as well as practical lectures to educationalists and student teachers on teaching handwriting.

Because he is a good, relaxed communicator his deft penmanship has been featured on television and he is frequently heard on radio discussing how to develop a good hand.

Starting Calligraphy is aimed at the beginner and touches on various aspects of calligraphy to help translate first attempts into a more permanent interest in the craft. Most of the work in the book has been written with a calligraphy fountain pen or dip pen.

As the reader acquires more skill and delves more deeply into the subject, increasing knowledge of materials and creative judgement will lead to a wish to experiment and produce work that is more professional in appearance.

Some of the examples of work featured in this book have been selected from entries to the 'Spirit of the Letter' competition for amateur calligraphers organised by Osmiroid.

CONTENTS

DELIGHT IN DISORDER ~ by Robert Herrick

A sweet disorder in the dress
Kindles in clothes a wantonness:
A lawn about the shoulders thrown
Into a fine distraction
An erring lace, which here and there,
Enthrals the crimson stomacher:
A cuff neglectful, and thereby
Ribbands to flow confusedly:
A winning wave (deserving note)
In the tempestuous petticoat:
A careless shoestring, in whose tie
I see a wild civility:
Do more bewitch me, than when Art
Is too precise in every part!

HOW TO BEGIN

Preparation

Calligraphy, or the art of beautiful writing, appeals to all ages. Most people can write, some better than others, and this fascinating craft simply makes use of a familiar subject, bringing to it a little more care and attention. With practise you can eventually produce all kinds of practical creations such as invitations, posters, greetings cards, labels, poems and certificates. It may even help to improve your handwriting.

An essential piece of equipment is a drawing board, which needs to be positioned so that it is at a right angle to the eyes, this avoids getting a distorted view of your work. Commercially produced boards are available using various methods to position the board at the required slope, but one can easily improvise with a piece of chipboard, plywood or thick card resting on your lap against a table.

Do not pin your work sheet to the board but hold it by a guard sheet (see illustration). Find your most suitable level for writing and then place your guard sheet over your practice paper and secure with drawing pins or masking tape. In this way you can ensure a constant level of writing, for as you complete each line you can raise the work sheet to your next line of writing. It also helps to protect your paper from any blemishes, stray ink or a build up of grease from your hands.

What You Will Need

If you are using a calligraphy fountain pen use only black ink especially made for fountain pens. Do not use waterproof ink as this gums up the nibs. An alternative type of pen to use is the traditional dip pen which has a small reservoir attachment. With the dip pen it is possible to use a wider variety of inks including gouache, which is a paint which can be thinned with water to ink consistency. During the early stages of practise it is advisable to keep to the ready made and free flowing types of ink, such as black fountain pen ink, or the non-waterproof carbon black ink.

All you need in addition to your pens and ink is a smooth, non-absorbant writing or drawing paper. The paper provided in a "layout" pad is suitable for practising letter shapes. A better quality paper is a smooth cartridge. It is such surfaced papers that allow you to make letters easily and rhythmically with a square edged nib.

Pad your writing sheet with a few sheets of blotting paper or cartridge paper, to cushion the harshness of the drawing board.

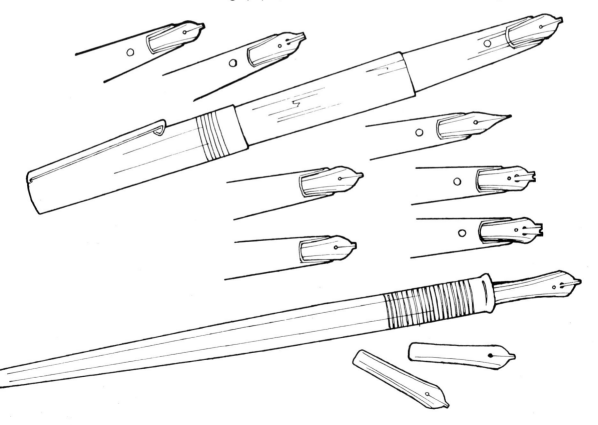

Getting Started

Commence by using a wide nib, say a B4 or B5, as this will give you more discipline over the hand and also clearly show up your mistakes!

Height of letters measured by nib widths.

Line spacing measured by letter heights.

When you have worked out the (nib width) height of your letters you will then need to rule some guide lines. A sharp H or HB pencil, soft eraser, set square and a ruler will then be needed. When ruling up for the small letters make sure to allow sufficient space for the ascending and descending strokes. A convenient measure is to put three small letter "O" shapes in between your lines of writing.

Guidelines can either be drawn straight onto your work sheet with a pencil or put onto a separate sheet of paper with a black fibre tip, in this form they can be used over and over again by placing them underneath your practice paper for every new page of writing.

Sit in a comfortable position at a table with reasonable light. Before beginning to write you should practise holding the pen and controlling it correctly. The pen must be held between the thumb and forefinger and should rest on the middle finger. It should be held consistently at an angle of 30 degrees or 45 degrees to the writing line as indicated for each style. This is one of the most difficult details for a beginner to master. Before starting to write any letters get used to manipulating a square edged writing instrument by making some basic strokes which are relevant to the skill of calligraphy, such as vertical, diagonal, horizontal and circular strokes. Try to keep the pen at the same angle. If you have any problems acquiring this technique, try a freely drawn scribble like pattern, endeavouring to keep the pen at a constant slope, in whichever direction it is travelling.

An exercise to help keep pen at a constant angle.

Basic strokes used for constructing letters.

Use the whole hand to manipulate the pen, not just the thumb and forefinger. If you find your fingers become cramped, it means you are gripping the pen too tightly. Try to relax your hold to obtain a sensation of gliding over the paper, rather than using the pen to furrow into the surface!

The best seated position for writing is with feet flat on the floor, with your back slightly leaning towards the desk. The paper should be set straight and immediately in front of you on the writing surface.

Layout

It is one thing to be able to inscribe a well proportioned letter, but the final test of one's calligraphic skill is to be able to present words in a balanced way as well as giving pleasure to the eye. This applies from a straightforward no smoking sign to a many versed poem or scroll.

To gain some idea of calligraphic effects it is worth looking at books which show examples of good layout, and even copying one or two to see for yourself how the balance of words is achieved. Here are some main points for you to consider:-

Start with simple layouts where words are balanced equally each side of a centre line, whether the paper is placed in a vertical or horizontal position.

To keep the eye's attention, and to avoid wandering off the edge of the paper, always allow a margin of space around the text or message. Slightly vary the ratio of the top, side and bottom spaces so that you obtain a feeling of balance.

Start with simple layouts where words are balanced equally each side of a centre line, whether the paper is placed in vertical or horizontal position.

Even when writing just one or two words, to create a feeling of balance it is necessary to place them slightly above the centre line to counter the illusion of the words appearing to float into the bottom half.

When designing a piece of calligraphy try to obtain a contrast somewhere in the layout by emphasising the word(s) which convey the purpose of the message. This can be done by size and colour, or both. Not only does this encourage the reader to stop and look, but it adds interest to the design.

It is almost impossible to complete a layout and get it right first time. To avoid wasting time and materials prepare your final piece of work by a trial and error process. Write out the required information as best as you can see it in your mind's eye. This is called a first "rough". You will begin to see at once where it needs to be improved. Cut your layout into strips containing the main words or groups of words and then on a clean sheet of paper juggle them around until you feel you have obtained a balanced design.

Contrast in size or colour makes a more interesting balance.

No contrast makes a less interesting balance.

Trial and error method for spacing a layout.

As your experience increases you will eventually find that you will be able to compose your layouts with a minimum of trial and error.

Every piece of work has new space problems to solve, and as you begin to see words as visual patterns you will want to try a variety of layouts to avoid creative stagnation. For instance the poem illustrated on page 4 is more attractive to the eye than if the lines were straight across the page. If you would like to experiment in this way start by cutting a piece of thin card with a subtly undulating line and then use it as a template to draw a grid of guide lines on to your work sheet.

Another popular exercise is to write the alphabet or quotations in a series of concentric circles.

Right handers

Left handers

Left Handers

The alphabet we have inherited in the Western part of the world has, in the main, been developed by right handers, and the construction of letters is therefore in favour of such people.

The action of writing travels from the left to the right side of the page and, assuming that the pen is held correctly, the right hand will pull away from what is written.

For about 12 to 15 percent of individuals the brain decides that the left hand shall predominate. This means that the writing instrument has to be used in the opposite way to the right hander, in a pushing action.

The pushing action makes it difficult to see what is being written and leads to smudging, especially when inks of a liquid nature are used.

There is a saying in the Middle East that right handers are going in the direction from whence they have come, and left handers are moving in the direction to which they are going!

To help left handers obtain success in calligraphy there are a few practical steps that can be taken to overcome the initial difficulties.

The most important aid to success is to use a left hand oblique nib. This allows the left hander to hold the pen without having to twist the hand and wrist into an awkward position.

Another tip worth trying is to place the paper at a slight angle to accommodate the pulling action.

An additional point so often forgotten is the source of light. In the case of left handers it needs to come from the right hand side to avoid any disturbing shadows.

The left hand oblique nib allows the left hander to hold the pen without having to twist the hand and wrist into an awkward position.

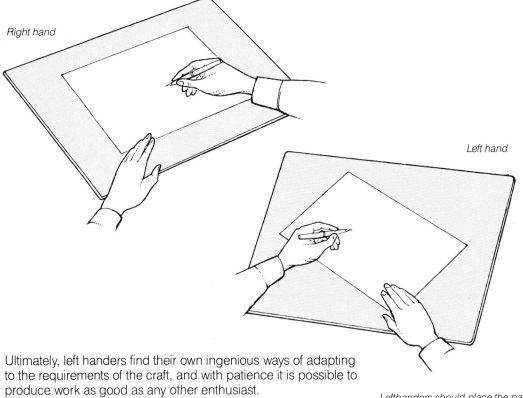

Right hand

Left hand

Ultimately, left handers find their own ingenious ways of adapting to the requirements of the craft, and with patience it is possible to produce work as good as any other enthusiast.

Lefthanders should place the paper at a slight angle and also make sure the source of light comes from the right hand side.

BASIC CALLIGRAPHY STYLES

There are a number of alphabets in use in the world, but the three main systems are the Far Eastern brush influenced styles, the Arabic forms of the Middle East, and our own Western tradition which was brought to maturity by the Romans and calligraphically continued and developed by the medieval scribes, until superceded by the technology of printing.

To appreciate the art of calligraphy we naturally return to these roots and the following pages introduce the chief styles which grew out of the period of handwritten books.

Roman

Western standards of legibility are based upon the Roman alphabet and this is the starting point from which to develop a knowledge of calligraphy. It is sometimes referred to as the "Foundational Hand", because if practised and mastered first then success in other styles will be more easily achieved. The term "Roman" includes the upright capitals and small letters as well as the sloping Roman Italic capitals and small letters.

Nib width height of capitals can be either 6 or 7 widths, and small letters 4 to 4½ nib widths.

30°

This alphabet looks at its best when the pen is kept at approximately 30° to the writing line. Do not over exaggerate the small finishing serifs at the beginning and end of the strokes or give them a wavy look.

abcdefghijk

lmnopqrstu

vwxyz 12345

67890

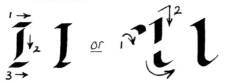

Capital slab serifs. Do not make them too large or over flourish.

not

Small letters. Alternative serifs. You can use either a slab serif or a 'beak and hook' finish.

or

IN the Begir
was the Wo
and the Wor
with GOD ar
Word was Go

The sun came up upon the left,
Out of the sea he came!
And he shone bright, and on the right
Went down into the sea.

From 'The Rime of the Ancient Mariner' by Samuel Taylor Coleridge

IF I CAN SPEAK
WITH THE TONGUES OF MEN
AND OF ANGELS
BUT HAVE NOT LOVE
I AM A BLARING TRUMPET
OR A CLANGING CYMBAL

CORINTHIANS

Examples of layouts showing the use of both the small and capital alphabets of the "Foundational" hand.

The Growmore Garden Centre, Flower-Bed Lane, Romsey · 1989 · Official opening by Lady Flora Gardener, April 30th

SPRING SUMMER AUTUMN WINTER

SISTER GEORGE

*From the Osmiroid **'Spirit of the Letter'** calligraphy competition for amateurs.*
A circular design which illustrates the decorative qualities of pen drawn letters, especially when coloured inks are used on a contrasting background.

Roman Formal Italic

This style was used by the Papal administration offices during the 16th century. When written formally it was used for books, but when written quickly it became a very practical hand for everyday correspondence (see page 34/35).

The letters are slightly narrowed and are given a forward slope of about 5°. Some beginners find it difficult to keep a consistent slope. An aid which can help to overcome this problem is to draw a grid of sloping lines with a black fibre tip, on a separate sheet of A4 paper, and then to place it underneath your layout practice paper. Mark off spaces at the top and the bottom of the sheet of 3 cm distance and then draw lines linking them together as shown in diagram.

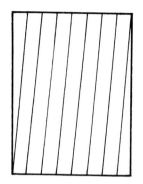

A grid of sloping lines will be a useful aid to obtain a consistant slope.

In the hands of a skilled person this style can be written in a very fluent manner, giving vitality to a piece of calligraphy.

Nib width height of capitals 8 nib widths, and small letters 4½ to 5 nib widths.

a b c d e f g h i j k l

m n o p q r s t u v w

x y z 1 2 3 4 5 6 7 8 9 0

A practical use for the formal italic style.

When to the session
sweet silent though
summon up remen
of things past, I sigh
lack of many a thi

Rise up my love, my fair one
and come away.
For lo, the winter is past.
The rain is over and gone.
The flowers appear on the earth.
The time of the singing of birds is come

Here in this sequestered close
Bloom the hyacinth and rose.
Here beside the modest stock
Flaunts the flaring hollyhock.
Here without a pang one sees
Ranks, conditions and degrees.

Season of mist and mellow fruitfulness,
Close bosom friend of the maturing sun.
Conspiring with him how to load and bless
With fruit the vines that round the thatch-eves run.
To bend with apples the moss'd cottage trees
And fill all fruit with ripeness to the core.

The winter comes
the frozen rut
Is bound with silver bars,
The snow-drift heaps against the hut
And night is pierced with stars.

MARGARET CHAPMAN

*From the Osmiroid **'Spirit of the Letter'** calligraphy competition for amateurs.*
A colourful and lively interpretation of the 'Seasons' theme, using light coloured washes to create a background effect for the calligraphy.

The ruling planet of Pisces is Neptune and it is a water sign. Positive traits include kindness, charity, creativity and intuition but negative traits are deceptiveness, lack of self-confidence and weakness of character.

SUE GUNN

*From the Osmiroid **'Spirit of the Letter'** calligraphy competition for amateurs.*
An example of work which demonstrates an acceptable blending of Roman brush drawn letters with a pen written text. The delicate use of colour adds to its eye appeal.

Roman Swash Letters

An attractive feature of the Roman formal italic style is that by extending some of the letter strokes and using vigorous flourishes, it can introduce a decorative note to a dull monotone page of writing. Flourishing letters is not as easy as it looks and requires a great deal of practise before they can be written with spontaneous confidence. The Victorian Copperplate copy books offer helpful inspiration on flourishes, and to develop the essential freedom of hand try copying some of them on newsprint with a calligraphy fibre tip before attempting to use a pen.

Black Letter or Gothic

This style began to emerge in the 12th century. It has been suggested by historians that the shortage of vellum (animal skin) for writing led to the scribes having to narrow the letters in order to fit more words onto the page. Whatever the reasons for the development of this alphabet it eventually became the accepted hand for manuscripts, predominating in Northern Europe.

To the professional scribe the term "Black Letter" is used to denote the many different examples of this style which are generally angular and characterised by the narrow spaces between the strokes. In order to obtain this effect when constructing the small letters, make sure that the white space inside the letter shape is about the same width as the pen stroke.

Nib width height of capitals 6 nib widths, and small letters 4 nib widths.

This style is noted for its decorative quality rather than its legibility, so use it carefully.

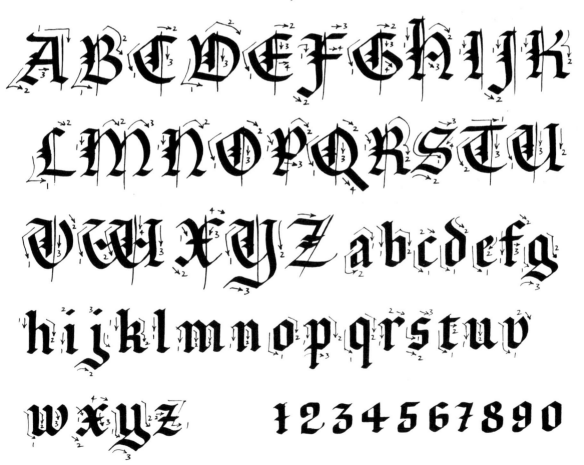

eason of mists and mellow fruitfulness.
Close bosom-friend of the maturing sun:
Conspiring with him how to load and bless
With fruit the vines that round the thatch-eaves run:
To bend with apples the moss'd cottage-trees.
And fill all fruit with ripeness to the core
To swell the gourd, and plump the hazel shells
With a sweet kernel; to set budding more.
And still more, later flowers for the bees.
Until they think warm days will never cease.
For Summer has o'er-brimm'd their clammy cells.

Who hath not seen thee oft amid thy store?
Sometimes whoever seeks abroad may find
Thee sitting careless on a granary floor,
Thy hair soft-lifted by the winnowing wind:
Or on a half-reap'd furrow sound asleep,
Drowsed with the fume of poppies, while thy hook
Spares the next swath and all its twined flowers:
And sometimes like a gleaner thou dost keep
Steady thy laden head across a brook;
Or by a cider-press, with patient look,
Thou watchest the last oozings, hours by hours.

Where the songs of spring? Ay where are they?
Think not of them, thou hast thy music too,—
While barred clouds bloom the soft-dying day,
And touch the stubble-plains with rosy hue;
Then in a wailful choir the small gnats mourn
Among the river sallows, borne aloft
Or sinking as the light wind lives or dies;
And full-grown lambs loud bleat from hilly bourn;
Hedge-crickets sing; and now with treble soft
The redbreast whistles from a garden-croft
And gathering swallows twitter in the skies.

To Autumn.   by John Keats. Sept 1819

ROBERT GODWIN

From the Osmiroid **'Spirit of the Letter'** *calligraphy competition for amateurs.*
The Gothic Black Letter is an exceedingly difficult hand to master. Here is a praiseworthy example, which is well proportioned, and thoughtfully placed on the paper.

The **GORLESTON PSALTER** *(14th. century) BRITISH MUSEUM. This is a manuscript page written on vellum in the Black Letter style. The study of good historic manuscripts is the best source of inspiration for anyone aspiring to the art of calligraphy.*

ta hic michi mmistrabat.

Non habitabit in medio domus
mee qui facit supbiam: qui loquit
iniqua ñ direxit in conspectu oclorum meorum.

In matutino insiciebam omnes
peccores fre: ut dispderem de ciuitate
dñi omnes opantes iniquitatem.

Dñine exaudi
oroem meam: et
clamor meus ad
te ueniat.

Non auttas fa
ciem tuam a me: in quacumqz die
tribloz inclina ad me aurem tuam.

In quacumqz die inuocauero te
uelociter exaudi me.

Uncial

Uncials developed from Roman capitals. They were easier and faster to write and were used extensively for much of the early Christian literature.

When vellum became the chief writing material, scribes discovered that curved strokes came naturally on such a surface, and as further development took place one can observe the beginnings of our present reading alphabet with the formation of ascenders and descenders.

Uncials were a transitional stage in the development of the alphabet as they were really a mixture of capitals and small letters. Today we tend to rationalise these two forms and present them as uncial capitals and small letters, although many of the letters in both versions are interchangeable. The illustrated alphabets are a modern adaption of this historic hand.

The pen is held so that the square edged nib is almost horizontal to the writing line. This gives the letters a bold and chunky look and can bring a touch of elegance to a calligraphic design.

ABCDEFGHI

JKLMNOPQ

RSTUVWX

YZ & ?

Nib width height of capitals 5 nib widths, and small letters 3½ to 4 nib widths.

abcdefghij
klmnopqrs
tuvwxyz

1234567890

Jnautemcalidap
madehordeifarin
enr imulcoctum
Mitzatetprilliu
qua calida iubat

Freely drawn copy of an 8th century manuscript.

*From the Osmiroid **'Spirit of the Letter'** calligraphy competition for amateurs.*
A very competent piece of work, showing how visually attractive a well rendered Uncial hand can be, when used in an informal but balanced manner.

An ecclesiastical motif using uncial letters. For certain subjects the 'chunky' character of this hand is an ideal choice.

SHEILA CHRISTOPHER

*From the Osmiroid **'Spirit of the Letter'** calligraphy competition for amateurs.*
Another design which has tastefully used a Uncial inspired hand to achieve its overall decorative effect.

Copperplate Handwriting

This style of handwriting was originally engraved on copper plates and the loops and flourishes became so popular that quills began to be sharpened to a point instead of a square edge, in order to imitate these features. A thick stroke has to be obtained by exerting pressure on the down strokes. It was the accepted way of writing in the 19th century and in the early part of this century.

It was the first style of writing introduced in the state schools in 1870 and many of the older generation still write in this way. Much of the original character of this style of writing is rarely seen today, chiefly because the tempo of life has increased and there is less time to give attention to the pressured down strokes and the loops and flourishes, but when written in the traditional manner it can be a very attractive style.

It is not strictly a part of calligraphic history in the sense that it was an attempt to copy the engraver's tool and involved a different technique from using a square edged calligraphy nib.

In order to maintain an even slope to the right you can use a guide line as suggested for the Formal Italic alphabet on page 18, but at a slightly steeper angle of approx. 60°.

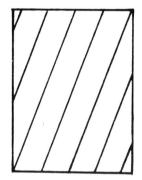

A grid of sloping lines will be a useful aid to obtain a consistent slope.

A B C D E F G H I J K

L M N O P Q R S T U

V W X Y Z a b c d e f

g h i j k l m n o p q r

s t u v w x y z

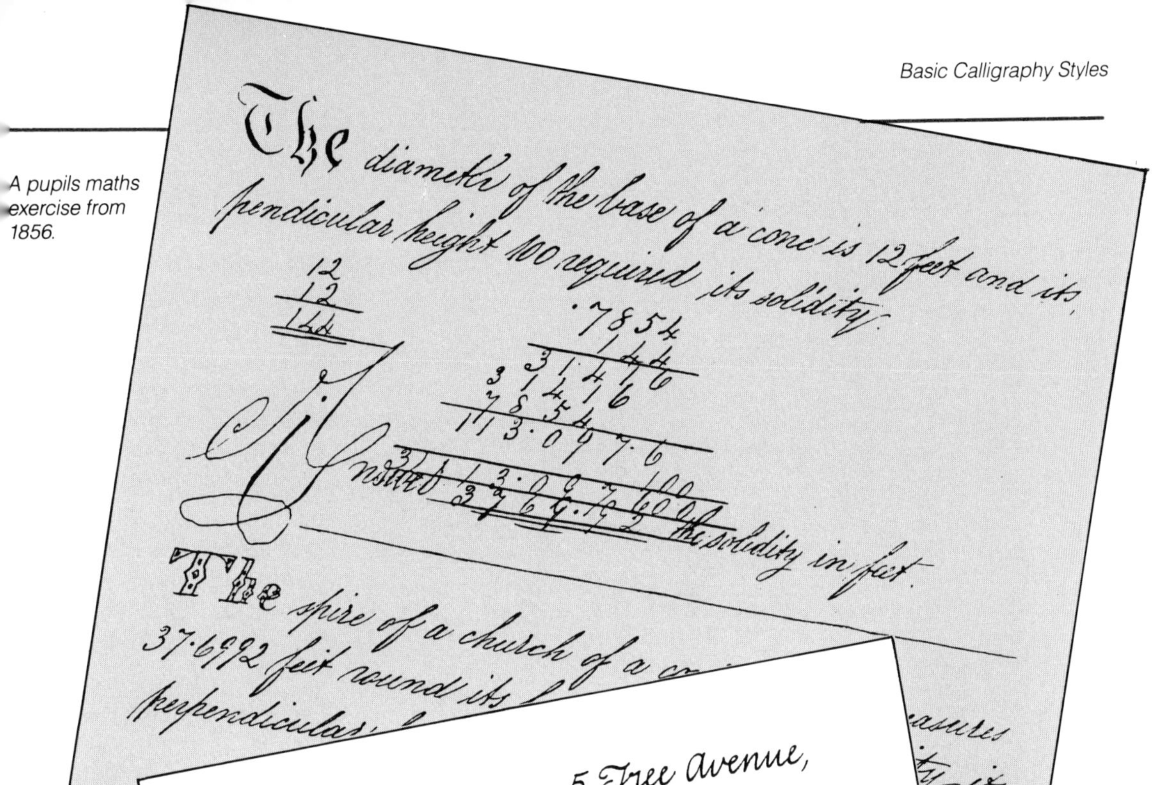

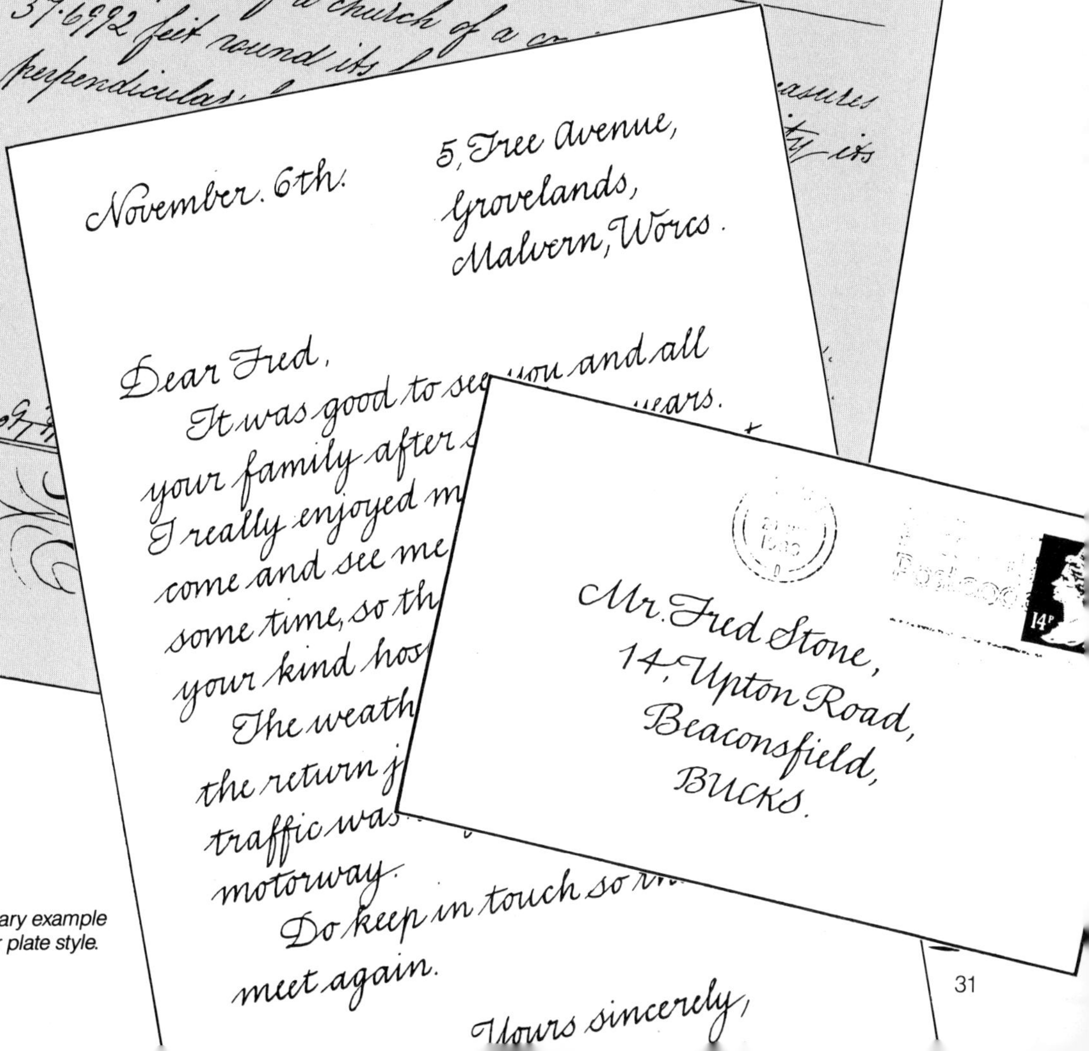

The diameter of the base of a cone is 12 feet and its perpendicular height 100 required its solidity.

12
12
144

·7854
144
31416
31416
7854
113·0976

Answer 113·0976 × 100 ÷ 3 = 37·6992 the solidity in feet.

The spire of a church of a co...
37·6992 feet round its b...
perpendicular ... measures
... ty its

A pupils maths exercise from 1856.

November. 6th.

5, Tree Avenue,
Grovelands,
Malvern, Worcs.

Dear Fred,
It was good to see you and all
your family after s... years.
I really enjoyed m...
come and see me...
some time, so th...
your kind hos...
The weath...
the return j...
traffic was ...
motorway.
Do keep in touch so ...
meet again.
Yours sincerely,

Mr. Fred Stone,
14, Upton Road,
Beaconsfield,
BUCKS.

A contemporary example of the copper plate style.

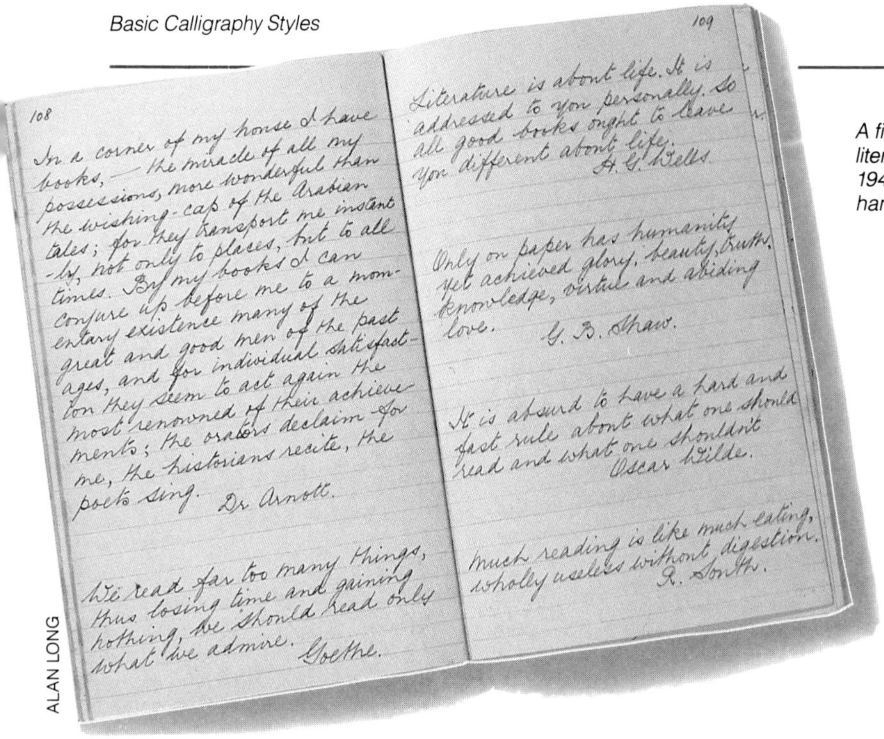

A fine example from a notebook of literary quotations collected during the 1940's shows the accepted style of handwriting during this time.

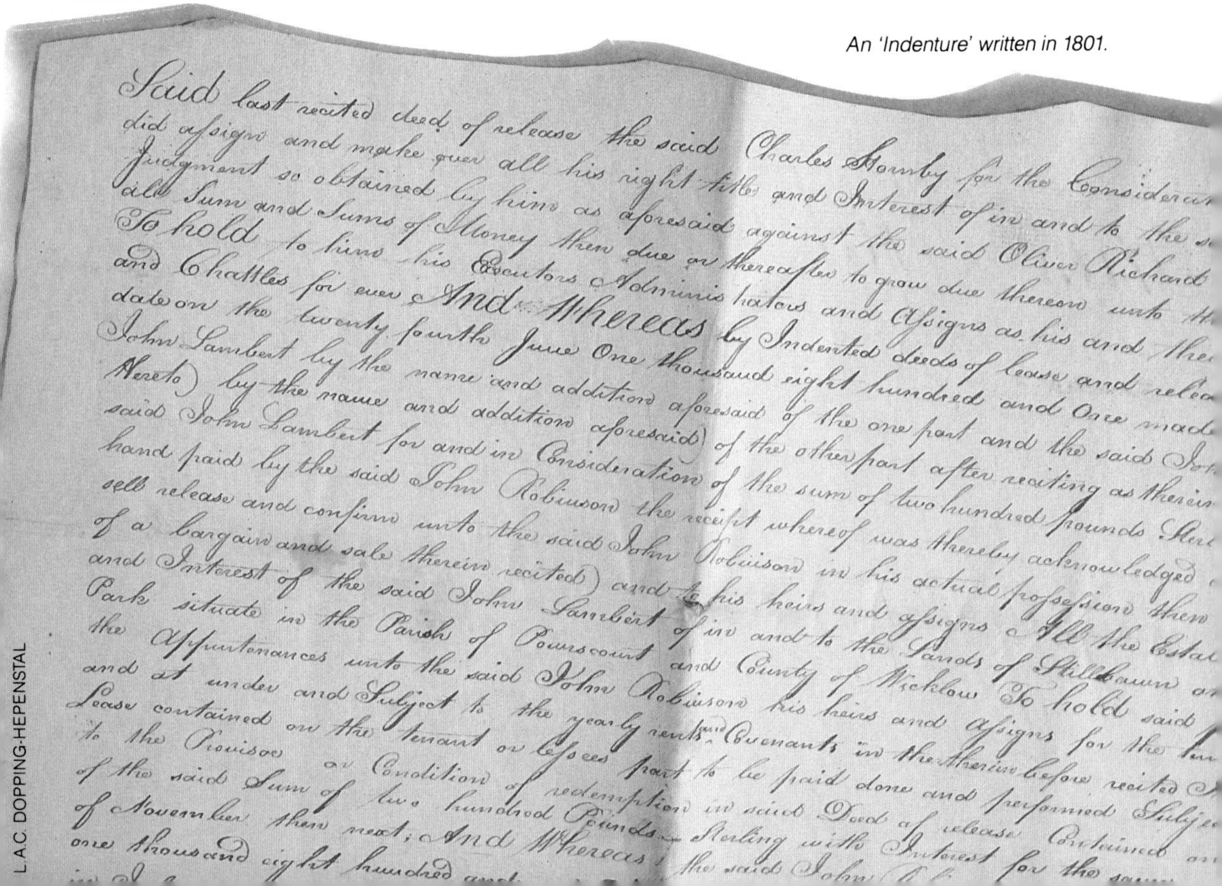

ALAN LONG

An 'Indenture' written in 1801.

L.A.C. DOPPING-HEPENSTAL

Whereas John Campbell
was on the 5ᵗʰ day of May Instant, Comm
to the House of Correction at Knutsford i
the County of Chester for One Month as a
Rogue and Vagabond. — We in consider
of Some Circumstances humbly represent
unto Us are Graciously pleased to extend
Grace and Mercy unto him, and to Gr
him Our Free Pardon for the Offence for
which he So Stands Committed as afores
Our Will and Pleasure therefore is that
you Cause him the said John Campb
to be forthwith discharged out of Custody

A 'Free Pardon' of 1847 shows the
attractive style of copperplate
handwriting showing the even slope to
the right.

NIGEL LONG

Italic Handwriting

This style is a more fluent version of the previous Roman formal italic alphabet. Most letters are formed with one continuous movement and can also be joined together as an aid to speed. Use an italic medium or broad nib unit and as with all calligraphy alphabets endeavour to keep the pen at a constant angle; in this case approximately 45°.

Keep your letters about five nib widths high and start by trying some basic rhythmic exercises.

The alphabet is easier to learn if practised in family groups of similar movement.

i t l u y c o a d g q e   n m r h b p k
v w x z f j s

The Diagonal Join. All letters in group 1 can be joined with a diagonal stroke to letters in groups 2, 3 and 4.

1. *a c d e h i l k m n u t*
2. *i j m n r p s t u v w x y*
3. *b h f l k*
4. *c a g d q o*

This shows how you join with a diagonal stroke to the letters in group 2, 3 and 4.

a aj u | a ah u | a aa v

hill kin many choice time liner climb her him mill diner nice

Words using the diagonal join

The Horizontal Join. There are five letters where a horizontal join is the most convenient way to join to the next letter. The numbered diagrams show you how this join is used.

f o t v w ˙fi oñ | 2. ol th | 3. oē vo

won moon for food whom tool ton vine nod thou hot town owl

Words using the horizontal join

Capitals. These are easier to learn if practised in groups of similar proportion.

OQCGUD HAVNTXYKZ

Elliptical   *Wide*

ILEFPBRSJ MW £?/:;"α

Narrow   *Extra Wide*

WALK GO STOP EXIT DOWN UP

Note: When first learning how to join do not join from these letters.

b g j p q r s x y z bun yes go exit ply

An example of the italic style of writing
written by an 11 year old pupil.

he Mole had been working very hard all the morning,
spring-cleaning his little home. First with brooms, then
with dusters; then on ladders and steps and chairs,
with a brush and a pail of whitewash; till he had
dust in his throat and ...es, and splashes of whitewash
all over his black fur, ... back and
weary arms. Spring
and in the earth '
penetrating even h
its spirit of divin
small wonder, t
his brush on t
also 'Hang sy
house witho...

A letter and envelope
written by an adult hand.

Riverside Education Centre.
Wye St. London. S.W.
Aug. 2nd.

Dear Mr. Barnard,
A short note to thank you
for all your stirling work at the
Centre last week.

good
who

another
...aps you
to
...ntually

London
20 JNE
1939

Mr Tom Barnard,
C/O OSMIROID INTERNATIONAL,
Fareham Road, Gosport,
Hants, PO13 0AL.

Yours sincerely.

KINGS LYNN
26 V 89
NORFOLK

12½

RR20628

Thomas Barnard Esq
S.S.1.
97, Bandley Rise
STEVENAGE .
Hertfordshire

16.2.87

Dear Mr. Barnard,

Thank you very much for
arrived recently - totall
My experience with Osmiroid pens yo
when changing nib units was a distu
business! They've come a long way
notice that this set is with "imp
I must admit that I haven't h
that direction in the past - pe
I use Osmiroid all the time
and layout. They corresp
ie. EF - 5, FINE - 4, M -
I have a set of nibs wh
uncial & I've taken a
for very small italic
All in all, I thin

Milefield Middle School, Grimethorpe, Nr.
23rd. November 1973.
Home: Barnsley 711344

School:

Dear Tom,
Many thanks for your letter of the 5th.
forgotten the arrangement. I suspected t
something had cropped up to prevent you
contacting me on your visit to South Yor
Perhaps when you are up this way again and
more time, you could give me a ring.
Incidentally, Mr. Gannon and I have been
to run the Middle School Course again at
Chichester so we may see you there next year
At present, I am in the process of judging the
S. I. H. 1973 Handwriting Competition. Quite
a task!

Yours sincerely,
Brian Walker.

Shadow Calligraphy

When you have acquired some skill at manipulating a calligraphy pen then you can begin to experiment with different kinds of nibs or square-edged writing instruments. One unique effect can be obtained by using a "Shadow" nib which draws two lines in one go. It is possible to spend many hours simply trying out different shadow nib effects, which although not of immediate use can be incorporated into future work. The following pages will give you some ideas to work from, but you can further your interest by obtaining some theme books on subjects such as flowers, sea fauna and cloud formations, and use them as a source of inspiration for interpreting natural forms into shadow nib designs.

A shadow nib can add extra sparkle to a page of calligraphy and is a useful method of drawing attention to a message. It is advisable not to fill the page completely using this type of nib, reading a mass of words formed with a double line can be very trying for the eyes.

Use smooth paper when working with this kind of nib. If you experience a "digging in" sensation, either you are pressing too much or using a rough surfaced paper.

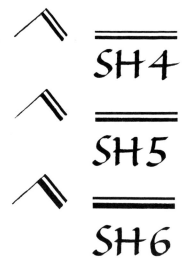

SH4

SH5

SH6

Shadow nibs

This alphabet is based upon the 'Foundational' hand. (Pages 14/15)

A design for a sticker showing how a shadow nib can be used, and yet not dominate the main message.

YOU ARE INVITED TO AN EXHIBITION OF PAINTINGS · ORGANIZED BY THE RED CROSS ·

in aid of the

ETHIOPIA FAMINE RELIEF

in the Plymouth Town Hall

MONDAY TO FRIDAY
JULY 1st - 5th

9 A.M. - 4 P.M.

An interesting effect can be obtained by using a white ink on a dark background.

Master the ARTS

ABCDEFGHIJKLM &?!

abcdefghijklm 123456

This alphabet is based upon the Formal
Italic hand, (Pages 18/19).

A
Merry Christmas
and a
Prosperous New Year

Silent Night

Sing
Sing
Sing

Carol
Song
Sheet

O three Kings · come all ye faithfull · Hark the herald angels sing · While shepherds watched their flocks by night · We

Get me
to the on time

Calligraphy designs using a shadow nib

Shadow Calligraphy

Flourishes

Flourishes can give a lively appearance to a calligraphy design, expecially when a shadow nib is used. To give yourself the experience of being able to flourish the pen, place a sheet of layout paper over the above design, secure onto page with paper clips and trace over the shapes with a calligraphy pen or fibre tip.

In this way you will gain some feeling of the process. When you have traced over the shapes a few times then try making your own exercise of flourishes on a separate sheet of paper.

The following page will show you some more interesting ways of using a shadow nib and suggest further ideas to you.

Borders

Plant designs

Patterns

Motifs

MAKING PENS

Although a wide range of ready made calligraphy products are available for a satisfactory introduction to the craft, your interest can be expanded by attempting to make your own pens. These can range from the rough and ready through to the ultimate refined quill pens.

In practise, any object or material which will retain ink and is shaped with a square edge can be used for calligraphic effect, such as a piece of thick felt held in a bulldog clip, a piece of balsa or matchbox wood pushed into a slot at one end of a piece of dowelling, a strip of bamboo cut with a square tip, square shaped crayons and chalks, a traditional carpenter's pencil, a square edged brush and some types of plastic can be cut and shaped like a calligraphic nib. All these ideas are worth experimenting with and within their limitations can produce some visually attractive results.

To avoid using up too much valuable paper, expecially if your pen produces a wide line, carry out your experiments on newsprint or wallpaper lining, using ordinary fountain pen ink or coloured dyes.

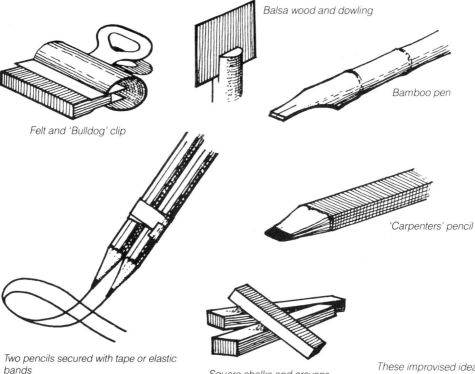

Balsa wood and dowling

Bamboo pen

Felt and 'Bulldog' clip

'Carpenters' pencil

Two pencils secured with tape or elastic bands

Square chalks and crayons

These improvised ideas for obtaining a calligraphic effect is a practical and attractive way of introducing young people to the nature of the craft.

Quills

For many centuries the quill ruled supreme in its influence on handwritten manuscripts and they were still in use by the end of the 19th century.

Large flight feathers

They were chosen from the large flight feathers of various types of birds such as the goose, swan, crow and turkey and professional scribes still consider there to be no substitute for writing on vellum. Quills can be bought commercially or sources of supply can be traced by anyone keen enough to search for them.

Quills need to be cured before they can be used for writing and there are various ideas on the best way to achieve this. Some say leave them to dry out naturally for about a year, others cure by the age-long method of plunging them into hot sand. It has even been suggested that leaving them in a hot oven after a Sunday dinner or for a few minutes in a microwave oven will give the desired results. If you seriously want to try using a quill for writing it would be wise to consult a specialist book, but it is possible to gain the experience of making a quill pen by obtaining a quill knife, scalpel, or craft knife, and making sure that the quill in question has dried out a little. The sequence of cutting actions is illustrated in the diagrams.

1. *First cut*

2. *Shape sides*

3. *Make slit*

4. *A sloped cut*

5. *A vertical cut*

Quill knife

For a correct hand balance make the quill approx 7 to 8 inches (17 to 20cm) in length.

A small but practical piece of advice when using a quill is to strip the feathers away from the stem. As romantic and photogenic as this detail appears to be, for a prolonged session of writing, they are useless and visually distracting. Although writing with quills is now a part of communication history we are, nevertheless, still the inheritors of the working principles which governed the scribe, in that our reading type faces and the general layout of books continue to follow the functional 'rules' developed by these ancient craftsmen.

For an appreciation of good calligraphy we cannot do better than study the surviving historical manuscripts. Rare examples can be seen in a few cathedrals or libraries, but the best collection is to be found in the British Museum in London. If you are inspired to increase your knowledge of this subject, this is an area of study you may wish to pursue.

An illustration from a 15th. century manuscript. This records the kind of tools, materials and environment in which medieval scribes worked. Note the sloped desk, the triangular weight to keep the vellum flat, the supply of ink at side of desk, and another desk to hold books for copying.

CALLIGRAPHY PATTERNS AND FLOURISHES

The graduating line produced by a calligraphy nib creates a pattern in its own right and a simple zig-zag movement across the page is at once more attractive than the same pattern written, say, with a ball pen. The freely drawn flourish is also of more interest to the eye as a result of this varying thickness of line.

This characteristic feature can be exploited by making repeat patterns for borders, informal pattern shapes or even for drawing symbols and pictures, as well as extending the shapes of letters to create decorative flourishes. A calligraphy nib used in this way will blend more readily with your work and give unity to your designs.

PEN PATTERNS

where appropriate

are decorative and

visually appealing

The skill of calligraphy gives the enthusiast an opportunity to exploit the use of the square edged nib, in creating endless variations of pen patterns.

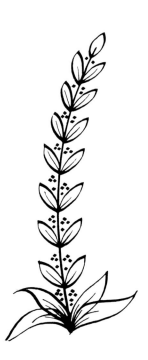

Makng sketch book observations from nature is a marvelous source of inspiration for creating calligraphic designs.

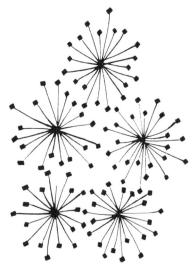

When using a calligraphy nib for drawing, eliminate the detail and simply go for the essential shape of the subject otherwise your drawings will look too cluttered.

Calligraphy used for commercial purposes presents another occasion when the pen drawn flourish can enliven the layout.

Experiment with letters, combining them into a balanced design. These letters are inspired by the Versal alphabet.

Anniversaries and the special occasion gives the calligrapher an opportunity to use the judicious flourish.

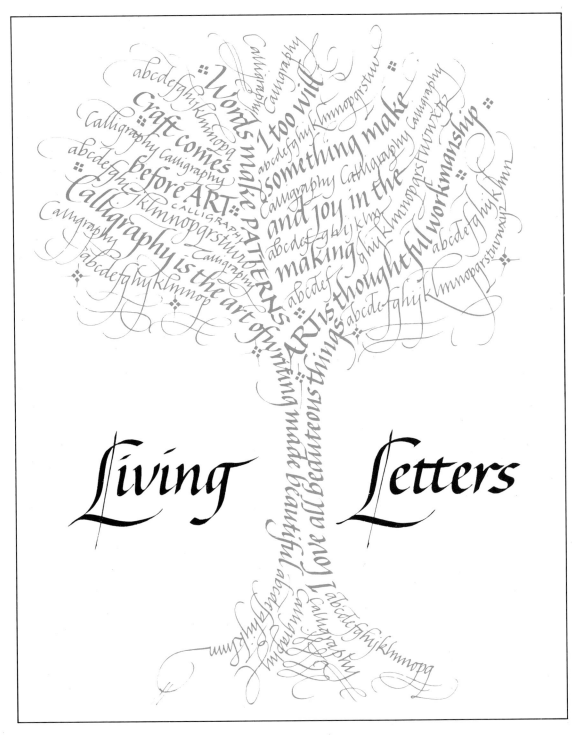

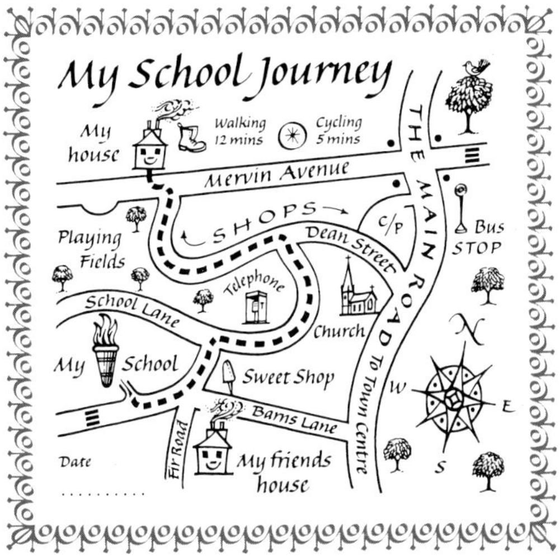

My School Journey

My house — Walking 12 mins — Cycling 5 mins

Mervin Avenue

THE MAIN ROAD

Playing Fields

SHOPS →

C/P — Bus STOP

Dean Street

School Lane

Telephone

My School

Sweet Shop

Church

To Town Centre

N
W — E
S

Date
....

Fir Road

Barns Lane

My friends house

PRACTICAL USES
OF CALLIGRAPHY

Letter Writing and Envelopes

One does not usually associate writing letters and addressing envelopes with formal calligraphy, but as a great deal of personal correspondence is still handwritten, especially for the annual round of anniversaries, birthdays and Christmas, it does give an opportunity for those who are interested in calligraphy to exercise their skill in presenting words in an attractive way.

Handwritten information is usually associated with the expression of one's personality. In its extreme form this means that it ceases to be legible, when it becomes the ideal ground for graphologists to forage in, but there seems to be no good reason why handwriting cannot both be expressive as well as readable. Knowledge of calligraphy, and the use of a good handwriting style, (Pages 34-37) or (Pages 30-33), can make you more sensitive to these details enabling you to give a letter or an envelope an added quality or visual appeal.

Putting thoughts on paper and addressing an envelope are useful exercises for developing rule of thumb judgements about placing a set number of words within a given space. There is scope for using coloured ink or paper to match your mood, or the character of the person you are corresponding with!

Calligraphy Choices

As with most crafts, calligraphy needs a great deal of patience to master. It is possible to acquire some helpful knowledge from books and in the process absorb ideas as to what is considered a good calligraphic design, but for the beginner, the best way to learn is to practice. If it is possible to attend a class this will accelerate the rate of progress and your understanding of the craft.

When you have mastered the basic skills, rather than launching into ambitious projects which involve a lot of planning and use of colour, it is advisable to begin with simple pieces of work. You might try designing labels, menus, greeting cards, notices, recipes, personal bookplates, poems, quotations, seating plans, certificates. On the following pages are examples of calligraphy which will give you some ideas for subjects you could attempt, to develop your skills, further your enjoyment and bring a contemporary enthusiasm to an ancient craft.

The space on an envelope gives an excellent opportunity to try out your newly acquired calligraphy skills.

Miss Nancy Ling,
Riverside Mansions,
WEYMOUTH,
Dorset. W12 DH3.

Mr. John Outray
Quickton Avenue,
Southampton Hants,
SO6 BJ2.

Mr. Gordon Wilder
22, Mayflower Road,
Plymouth,
DEVON, PO3 H12

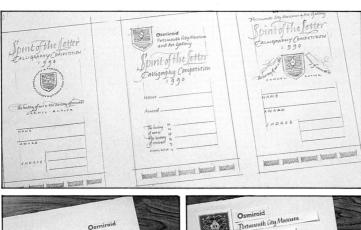

First, organise the words of the project by making some pencil 'roughs'.

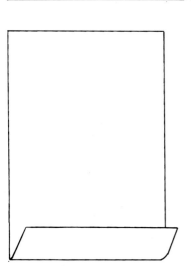

Write out the words with the nib widths, and in the colours you think will give you a balanced design, including any symbols, crests or pictorial additions. This is done without any reference to the final spacing by lining up the words from a single marginal line. Remember to give emphasis to the main elements of the subject.

Cut out the lines of calligraphy into separate strips.

Order the strips into the format you have chosen from your pencil 'roughs'. From this you will be able to decide whether you have made a particular detail too large or too small, or if any adjustments need to be made to the spacing.

Proceed to complete finished design and add lace tie-up ribbon.

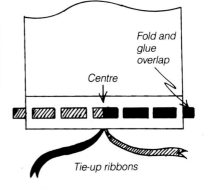

Fold paper at bottom of certificate.

Cut slits width of tape starting in centre.

Using two pieces of ribbon start lacing one piece through the centre slit and continue lacing to one end, leaving about a 2cm overlap which is glued between the two sheets of paper, also allow 20-30cm loose to tie-up. Lace second piece of ribbon the same way.

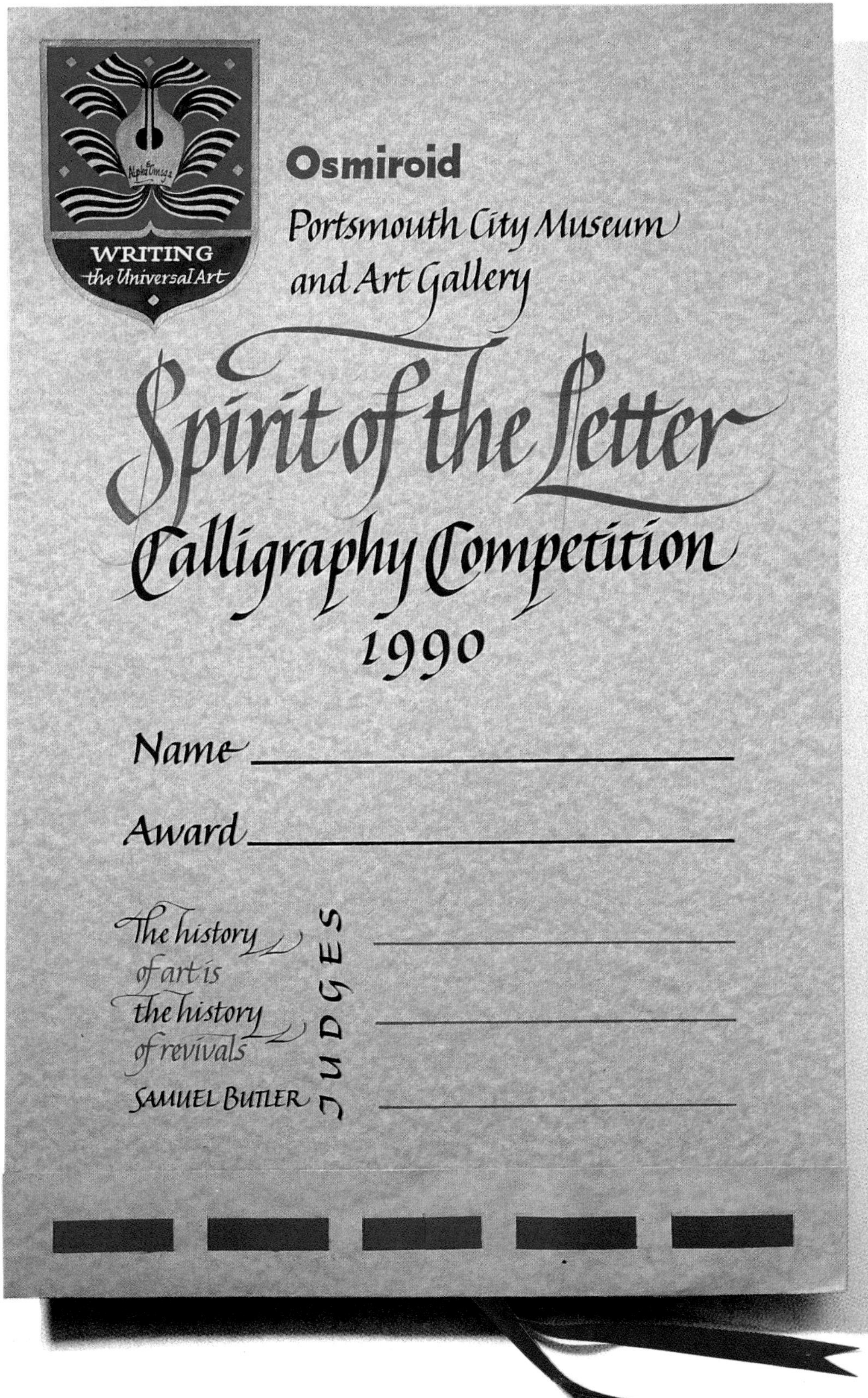

Osmiroid

WRITING
the Universal Art

Portsmouth City Museum
and Art Gallery

Spirit of the Letter
Calligraphy Competition
1990

Name _____

Award _____

The history
of art is
the history
of revivals

SAMUEL BUTLER

JUDGES _____

_____

_____

Here, and on the opposite page, are typical subjects you can attempt when you are ready to try your hand at a calligraphic design and layout.

They wish you a Joyous Christmas & a Good New Year

To wish you a Joyous Christmas & a Good New Year

presented Him with gifts of

opened their treasures &

gold & of incense & of myrrh

From the Harrison Family

JAMES WINSTANLEY

From the Osmiroid **'Spirit of the Letter'** calligraphy competition for amateurs.

This kind of subject is a frequent request for calligraphers to undertake. It needs to be easy to read, and attractive to look at. It also illustrates the importance of acquiring some ability at the added skills of drawing and using colour.

CLAIRE CORMACK

*From the Osmiroid **'Spirit of the Letter'** calligraphy competition for amateurs.*
An example of calligraphy which further illustrates the versatility of the alphabet when used in an imaginative way. The use of colour on a contrasting background, and original layout, all combine to make an eye catching design.

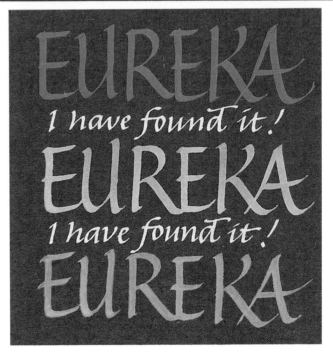

In between periods of practise, and whatever the level of attainment, continue experimenting with the use of colour. Not only do you continue to gain valuable experience in the craft, but the best results can always be integrated into future work.

The Osmiroid Creative Leisure Series

'Creative Leisure' sums up a range of products from Osmiroid - a series of kits, sets and books that provides you with all you need to make a start in a new craft.

Each of the Craft Kits comes complete with all the materials needed to start work and includes a full-colour illustrated book written by an expert in the subject. The book describes how to use the materials provided and leads you through the steps to creating attractive pieces of work. The Craft Kits are presented in a colourful case, so are also ideal as gifts. The kits are:-

- **Colour Calligraphy Kit**
- **Chinese Brush Painting Kit**
- **Pen and Ink Drawing Kit**
- **Pen and Ink Sketching Kit**
- **Poster Making Kit**
- **Stencilling Kit**

In addition, the Craft Books are available separately from bookshops and art material outlets. The titles are:-

- **Chinese Brush Painting** *by Pauline Cherrett*
- **Colour Calligraphy** *by Barbara Bundy*
- **The Art of Sketching** *by Malcolm MacDonald*
- **Pen and Ink Drawing** *by Jonathan Stephenson*
- **The Art of Poster Making** *by John Smith*
- **The Art of Stencilling** *by Helen Barnett*
- **Oriental Craft Painting** *by Pauline Cherrett*
- **A Course in Drawing** *by Malcolm MacDonald*
- **The Art of Illuminated Lettering and Heraldry** *by Barbara Bundy*

Also published by Osmiroid are:-

- **Starting Calligraphy** *by Tom Barnard*
- **Making Calligraphy Work For You** *by Tom Barnard and Christopher Jarman*

More Craft Kits are planned, so with a little help from Osmiroid a whole new world of creative leisure opens up.

Design and artwork by Nigel Long, Winchester